THAT'S DISGUSTING!

DISGUSTING HUMAN BODY

By Joanne Mattern

Kaleidoscope
Minneapolis, MN

Bigfoot Books

The Quest for Discovery Never Ends

....

This edition is co-published by agreement between Kaleidoscope and World Book, Inc.

Kaleidoscope Publishing, Inc.
6012 Blue Circle Drive
Minnetonka, MN 55343 U.S.A.

World Book, Inc.
180 North LaSalle St., Suite 900
Chicago IL 60601 U.S.A.

All rights reserved. No part of this book may be reproduced in any form without written permission from the publishers.

Kaleidoscope ISBNs
978-1-64519-252-7 (library bound)
978-1-64519-320-3 (ebook)

World Book ISBN
978-0-7166-4179-7 (library bound)

Library of Congress Control Number
2020936221

Text copyright © 2021 by Kaleidoscope Publishing, Inc. All-Star Sports, Bigfoot Books, and associated logos are trademarks and/or registered trademarks of Kaleidoscope Publishing, Inc.

Developed and produced by Focus Strategic Communications Inc.

Printed in the United States of America.

FIND ME IF YOU CAN!

Bigfoot lurks within one of the images in this book. It's up to you to find him!

TABLE OF CONTENTS

Chapter 1: Living Inside You 4

Chapter 2: Super Slime 10

Chapter 3: Tummy Troubles 16

Chapter 4: One End or the Other 22

Beyond the Book 28
Research Ninja 29
Further Resources 30
Glossary 31
Index 32
Photo Credits 32
About the Author 32

Chapter 1
Living Inside You

The human body is a pretty cool place. It's full of **organs** that allow us to think and move, hear and see. But our bodies are also really disgusting. Let's take a look at some of the disgusting things that are part of us.

Did you know your body is full of creepy-crawlies? That's right. Demodex mites live on the skin of your face. They live in your eyelashes, too. But don't panic or run to the doctor. These creatures live on everyone. And they usually aren't bad for you.

Mites are tiny. There may be more than 25 mites on one eyelash.

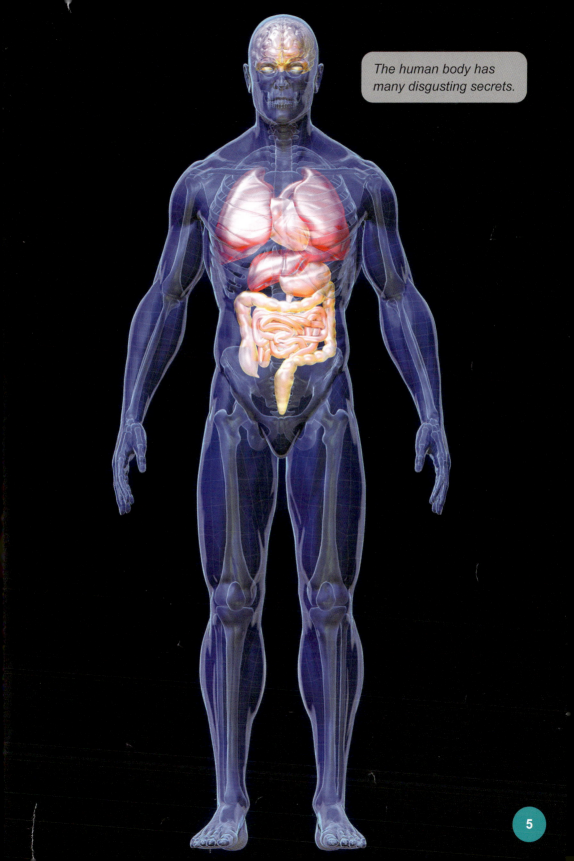

The human body has many disgusting secrets.

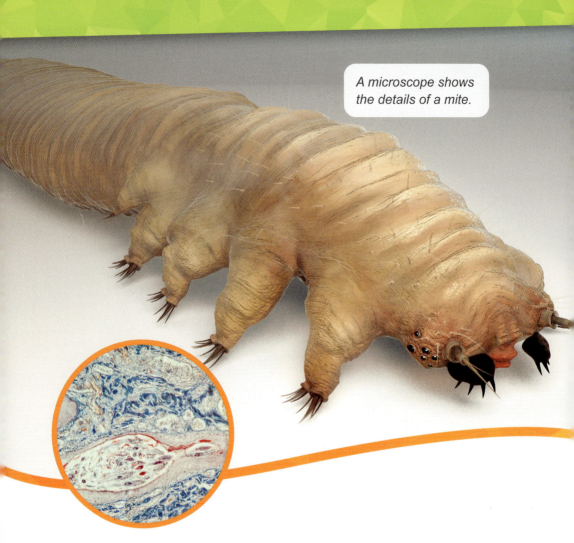

A microscope shows the details of a mite.

Mites are so small that you can only see them with a **microscope**. These tiny creatures have lots of legs. Adult mites live less than a week. But they pack a lot of disgusting life into those few days.

There are two kinds of Demodex mites. One kind lives in **pores** and hair **follicles**. The other lives deep in the oil **glands**. Most of these mites live on faces. But they can be found in other places on the body as well.

Why do mites live on our bodies? So they can find things to eat. Scientists aren't sure exactly what these mites eat. Some think they eat dead skin. Others think they eat **bacteria** that live on our skin. Some mites might eat the oil inside our glands. Aren't you glad that dead skin and oil aren't on your dinner menu?

FUN FACT
A mite was found in human earwax way back in 1842.

Too many mites can cause mange.

Demodex mites feed on dead skin cells.

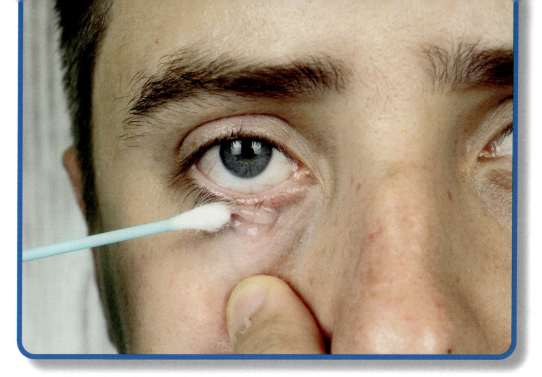

Demodex mites can live in the follicles at the base of eyelashes.

Here's something even more disgusting about mites. These creatures can't poop. Instead, they store up waste inside their body. When they die, their bodies dry up. All that poop leaks out onto your skin.

Mites certainly sound disgusting. People may get eye **irritations** from mites. But the news is not all bad. Usually these mites do not cause any harm. And even though almost everyone has them, most people never know it. They are just a fact of life on our bodies.

FUN FACT

Mites are most active while you are asleep. So while you're snoring, these little creatures are busy munching on your face.

Chapter 2
Super Slime

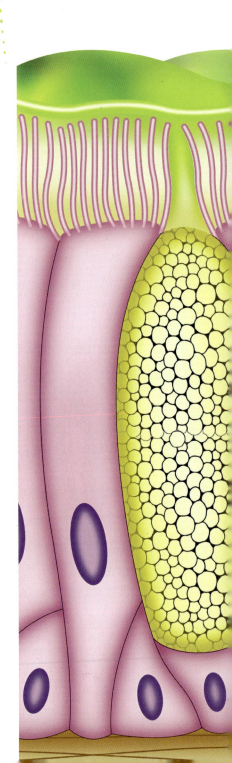

It's everywhere. It's in our noses and throats. It's in our **digestive systems**. What is this slimy, slippery stuff? It's mucus, and it's an important part of our bodies.

Mucus is produced by special glands all over the body. It is mostly made up of water. A normal person produces up to 1.5 quarts (1.5 liters) of mucus every day. And yes, we swallow a lot of it during the day. Yuck!

We may think mucus is gross. But it helps our bodies in many ways. This slimy goo keeps our bodies running smoothly.

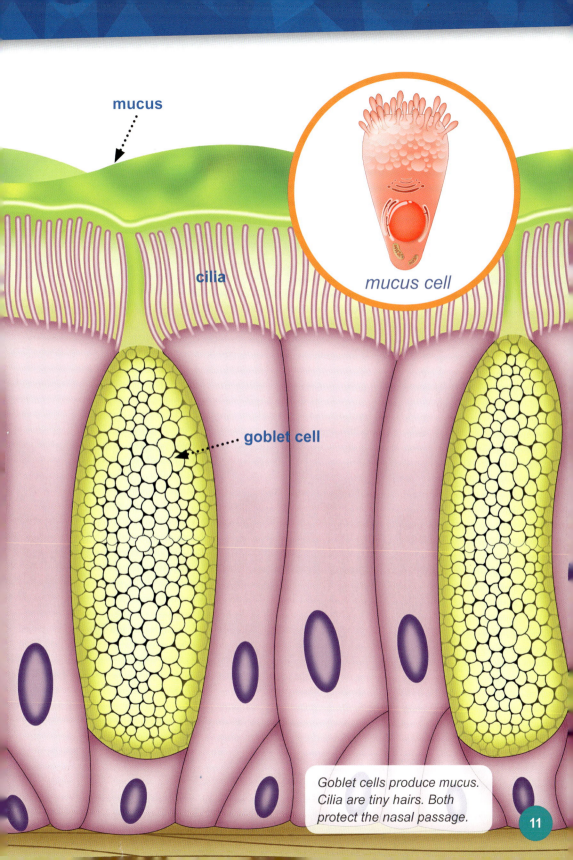

Goblet cells produce mucus. Cilia are tiny hairs. Both protect the nasal passage.

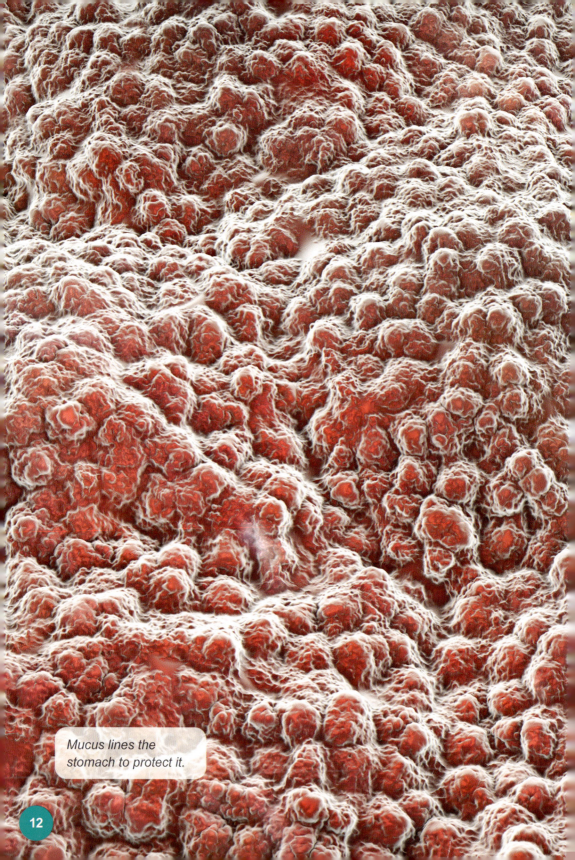

Mucus lines the stomach to protect it.

Mucus has many uses. It keeps our organs from drying out. It also helps things flow smoothly. For example, mucus helps food move through the digestive system. It also protects the stomach from acids that digest foods.

Mucus also protects us in other ways. Dirt and bacteria get trapped in mucus' sticky slime. This prevents them from getting into the lungs and making us sick.

When you have a cold, your nose runs a lot. That's because your body makes extra snot. Your nose will be stuffed up with lots of boogers, too. Don't pick them.

FUN FACT

Mucus is not the same as pus. Pus oozes out of an infection. But it's often green and gooey, just like snot.

Mucus helps to fight off bacteria and viruses.

Mucus is usually clear. But when someone is sick, the mucus changes color. The colors can provide clues about what is wrong.

If someone has an infection, mucus can be green or yellow. Those colors come from cells fighting the infection. So when you cough or sneeze up thick, colorful snot, you know your body is hard at work kicking that infection out the door.

Brown mucus contains blood. Don't panic. This is common when you have a cold.

Mucus helps keep our bodies running smoothly. That's not disgusting at all, right? Well, maybe.

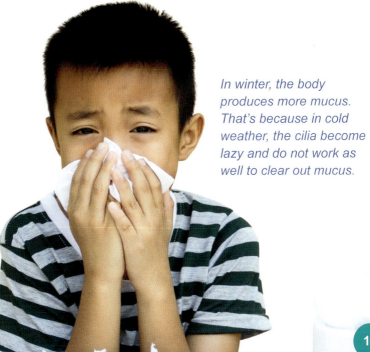

In winter, the body produces more mucus. That's because in cold weather, the cilia become lazy and do not work as well to clear out mucus.

Chapter 3
Tummy Troubles

Most people can digest just about any kind of food. That's because our stomachs are full of powerful digestive acid. This acid is strong and works hard. But it's also pretty nasty.

After you chew and swallow your food, it slides down a long tube into the stomach. That's when the stomach acid gets to work. The acid breaks down your last meal, whether it was pizza or vegetables or potato chips. Everything gets churned around into a disgusting, gloppy mess.

FUN FACT
A human stomach holds about seven ounces (198 gm) of acid.

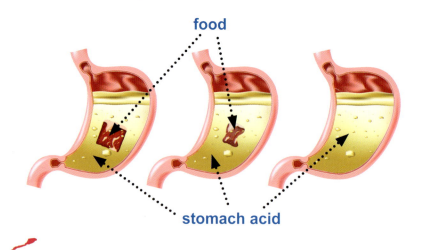

food

stomach acid

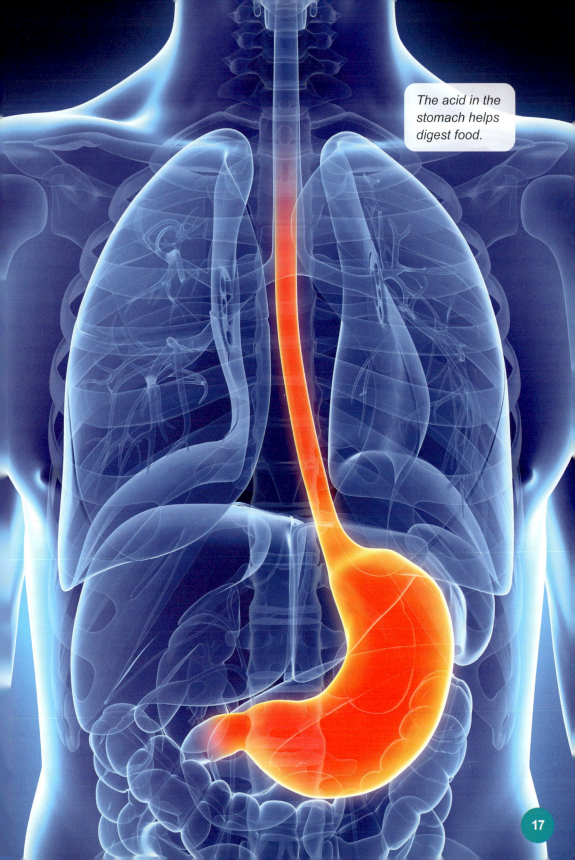
The acid in the stomach helps digest food.

THE PH SCALE

To do its job, stomach acid has to be really strong. Acid is measured on the pH scale. The lower the number, the stronger the acid. Stomach acid measures between one and three on the scale. That's stronger than vinegar. That's strong enough to break down metal. That's why the acid in your stomach can break down food so quickly.

Why doesn't that acid eat away at your stomach itself? A layer of mucus protects the stomach lining. That's right, along with acid, your stomach has lots of slime, too.

FUN FACT
Sometimes the mucus layer isn't thick enough to protect your stomach. That causes a hole in the stomach lining. That hole is called an ulcer, and it hurts.

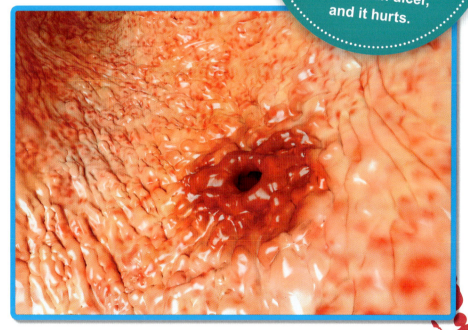

How long does it take for stomach acid to work? That depends on what you ate. Sugar breaks down quickly. Stomach acid can take care of candy or cookies in a short time. Proteins, such as meat, take longer. A meaty meal can take up to four hours to digest.

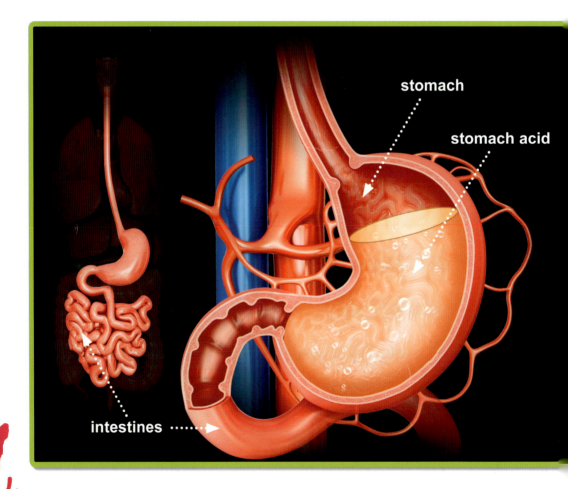

What if you eat something poisonous or rotten? Sometimes your stomach knows. It will get rid of it as quickly as it can. You might vomit up the nasty food. Or you might get a bad case of **diarrhea**. Either way, that nasty food is out of there.

Stomach acid doesn't just break down food. It **sterilizes** it. The acid is so strong, it kills bacteria and other harmful substances.

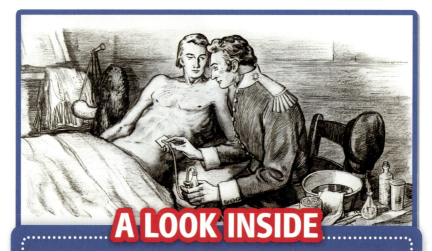

A LOOK INSIDE

In 1822, a fur trapper named Alexis St. Martin was shot in the stomach. He lived, but the hole in his stomach never closed. A doctor named William Beaumont made a deal with St. Martin. The trapper let Beaumont tie food onto a string. Then he lowered it into St. Martin's stomach. Dr. Beaumont's experiments helped scientists learn how stomach acid digests food.

Chapter 4
One End or the Other

Digestion is pretty simple. Food goes in one end. It comes out the other. However, sometimes food comes out the way it went in. When our stomachs reject food, we vomit. And there are few things as disgusting as vomiting.

People (and animals) vomit for many reasons. Sometimes we can't keep food down because we're sick. Bacteria can irritate the stomach and make it throw up food. Sometimes people vomit because they eat too much or too fast. There are many other reasons as well.

Some people think vomit smells like parmesan cheese.

HUMAN DIGESTIVE SYSTEM

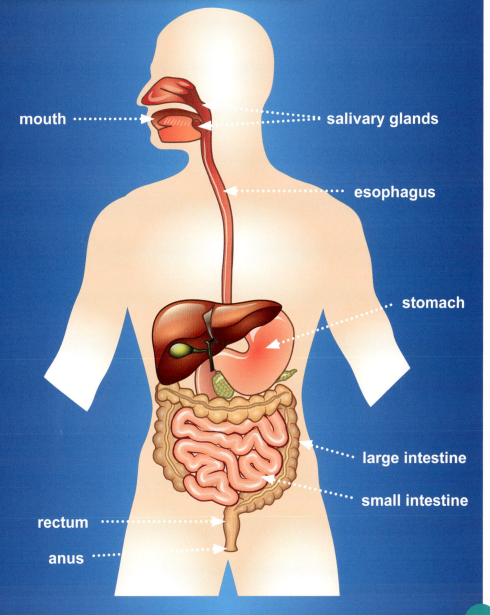

FUN FACT

People used to think ancient Romans ate so much that they would vomit and then eat more. They believed Romans had special rooms for puking. These rooms were called vomitoriums. However, this disgusting story is just a myth.

What is vomit, exactly? It is undigested food mixed with stomach acid and mucus. Vomit feels disgusting. It tastes and smells awful, too. However, it is the body's way of getting rid of food that our stomachs just can't handle.

It's much better for food to exit the body out of the other end. After we eat, food moves through the digestive system. All the nutrients and a lot of the water are removed so the body can use them.

Now just waste is left. It's time to go to the bathroom and poop it out.

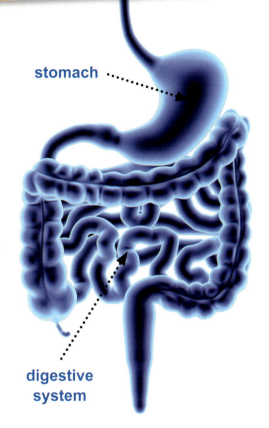

stomach

digestive system

In the end, some of our food ends up in the toilet.

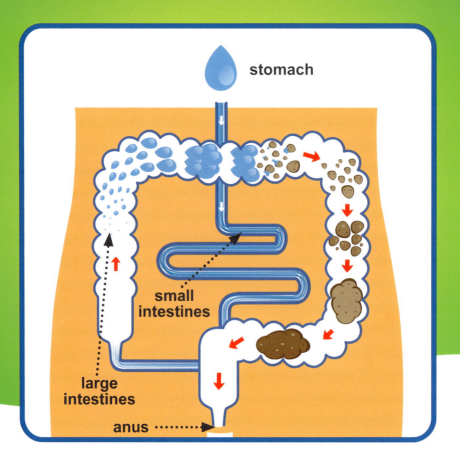

Food travels from the stomach to the small intestines, and then moves to the large intestines. Then, it comes out the anus as poop.

The large intestine is the last stop in the digestive system. After that, nothing is left but waste. That waste moves down into the rectum. It presses against nerves. That sends a signal that we need to poop.

Poop can include many things. There can be bits of undigested food. It also has bacteria and water. That bacteria is what makes poop smell so bad. Your poop's smell can change depending on what you ate as well.

Why is poop brown? It includes old red blood cells that the body doesn't need anymore. It can also include a digestive chemical called bile. Doesn't it feel good to flush all of that disgusting stuff away?

PASSING GAS

Sometimes our digestive systems needs to get rid of smelly gases. If these gases are in our rectums, we might let out noisy, stinky farts. If they're in the stomach, we'll rip out burps. If a person was trapped in a small space with no air, and they farted a lot, they could actually die. That's because the space would fill with gases. What a disgusting way to go.

BEYOND THE BOOK

After reading the book, it's time to think about what you learned. Try the following exercises to jumpstart your ideas.

THINK

WHAT'S INSIDE YOU? The human body is an amazing thing, but many of the things it does are gross and strange. What are the most unusual ways the parts of the body work together? What are some ways you can keep your body healthy?

CREATE

AMAZING YOU. Choose one organ or system in your body. Draw a poster or a flow chart to describe what that organ or system does and how it works.

SHARE

THAT'S GROSS. What do you think is the most disgusting thing about the human body? Research the topics in this book. Or find a new topic. Collect evidence that you think proves your choice is the grossest. Present your argument to a friend.

GROW

BIONIC BODIES. Some people say the body is like a machine. Science has created many bionic, or machine-powered, body parts. Research unusual ways that people make new parts for the human body. Create a video or a photo essay to show these medical wonders.

RESEARCH NINJA

Visit **www.ninjaresearcher.com/2527** to learn how to take your research skills and book report writing to the next level.

RESEARCH

DIGITAL LITERACY TOOLS

SEARCH LIKE A PRO
Learn how to use search engines to find useful websites.

FACT OR FAKE?
Discover how you can tell a trusted website from an untrustworthy resource.

TEXT DETECTIVE
Explore how to zero in on the information you need most.

SHOW YOUR WORK
Research responsibly— learn how to cite sources.

WRITE

GET TO THE POINT
Learn how to express your main ideas.

PLAN OF ATTACK
Learn prewriting exercises and create an outline.

DOWNLOADABLE REPORT FORMS

Further Resources

BOOKS

Macdonald, Fiona. *The Science of Snot and Phlegm: The Slimy Truth About Breathing*. New York, NY: Franklin Watts, 2018.

Perish, Patrick. *Disgusting Bodily Functions*. Minneapolis, MN: Bellwether Media, 2015.

Woolf, Alex. *You Wouldn't Want to Live Without Boogers!* New York, NY: Franklin Watts, 2017.

Woolf, Alex. *You Wouldn't Want to Live Without Poop*. New York, NY: Scholastic, 2016.

WEBSITES

Factsurfer.com gives you a safe, fun way to find more information.

1. Go to www.factsurfer.com.
2. Enter "Disgusting Human Body" into the search box and click 🔍
3. Select your book cover to see a list of related websites.

Glossary

bacteria: microscopic, single-celled living things that are found everywhere.

diarrhea: loose, liquidy poop.

digestive system: the arrangement of organs and chemicals that break down food in the body.

follicles: the small, deep holes, or openings in the skin, around the roots of hair.

glands: parts of the body that produce chemicals for the body to use or discard.

infection: an illness in part of the body caused by bacteria or a virus.

irritations: things that are painful or make the body uncomfortable.

microscope: an instrument that makes tiny objects look bigger.

organs: large parts of the body, such as the brain or lungs, that have a specific function.

pores: small openings in the skin that allow liquid, such as perspiration, to escape.

sterilize: to remove bacteria and make something clean.

Index

Beaumont, William, 21
Demodex mites, 4, 5, 6, 7, 8, 9
digestive system, 10, 13, 25, 26, 27
earwax, 7
eyelashes, 4, 9
farts, 27
gas, 27
infection, 13, 14
intestines, 20, 23, 26
mucus, 10, 11, 12, 13, 14, 15, 19, 24

pH scale, 18, 19
poop, 9, 25, 26, 27
pus, 13
Romans, 24
St. Martin, Alexis, 21
stomach acid, 16, 17, 18, 19, 20, 21, 24
ulcers, 19
vomit, 21, 22, 24

PHOTO CREDITS

The images in this book are reproduced through the courtesy of: SciePro/Shutterstock Images, front cover (top left), p. 17; Kalcutta/Shutterstock Images, front cover (center left), pp. 1, 6 (top); Alona Siniehina/Shutterstock Images, front cover (center right), p. 9; pathdoc/Shutterstock Images, front cover (bottom left), p. 3; OHishiapply/Shutterstock Images, p. 4; The beeeer/Shutterstock Images, p. 5; Dr. Norbert Lange/Shutterstock Images, p. 6 (inset); spline_x/Shutterstock Images, p. 7; NANOCLUSTERING/SCIENCE PHOTO LIBRARY/Getty Images, p. 8; ilusmedical/Shutterstock Images, pp. 10-11; Designua/Shutterstock Images, p. 11 (inset); KATERYNA KON/SCIENCE PHOTO LIBRARY/Getty Images, p. 12; Ketolina/Shutterstock Images, p. 13; Suwan Wanawattanawong/Shutterstock Images, p. 14; Thaweekeirt/Shutterstock Images, p. 15 (top); GUNDAM_Ai/Shutterstock Images, p. 15 (bottom); gritsalak karalak/Shutterstock Images, p. 16; BlueRingMedia/Shutterstock Images, p. 18; JUAN GARTNER/SCIENCE PHOTO LIBRARY/Alamy Stock Photo, p. 19; PIXOLOGICSTUDIO/SCIENCE PHOTO LIBRARY/Getty Images, p. 20; Bettmann/Getty Images, p. 21; Jan H Anderson/Shutterstock Images, p. 22; La Gorda/Shutterstock Images, p. 23; Monika Draaisma/Shutterstock Images, p. 24; Graphic Compressor/Shutterstock Images, p. 25 (top); Business stock/Shutterstock Images, p. 25 (bottom); Luciano Cosmo/Shutterstock Images, p. 26; What Is My Name/Shutterstock Images, p. 27 (top); CGN089/Shutterstock Images, p. 27 (bottom).

About the Author

Joanne Mattern is the author of many books for children. She loves to learn new things and especially enjoys anything disgusting or weird. Joanne lives in New York state with her family and pets, none of whom is disgusting.